I0503024

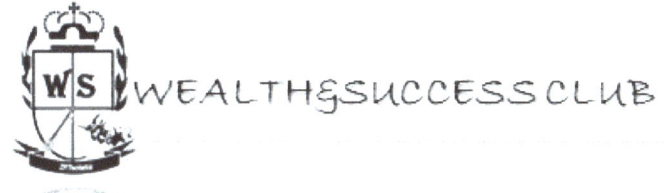

Advertising . Marketing . Selling

THE BUSINESS ART OF PERSUASION AND COMMUNICATION

Effective Powerful & Successful
Marketing, Advertising and Selling
Through Simple Words

WEALTH&SUCCESS CLUB

The Business Art of Persuasion And Communication

Effective, Powerful & Successful Marketing, Advertising & Selling

Copyright W&S Club (Wealth & Success Club). All rights reserved.

Contents

Copyright W&S Club (Wealth & Success Club). All rights reserved.

Introduction

The business art of Persuasion and Communication is an ebook that contains the most powerful words that brings successful Marketing, Advertising and Selling. Yes, these are definitely Power Words That Brings You Sales.

Congratulations for purchasing this ebook. Even though you may not realize it yet, obtaining this ebook is one of the smartest things you have ever done.

You will soon discover some proven words and formulas which are in use today by some of the most successful copywriters in the world.

As you read through the material, you will discover the secret power words and formulas which you can apply to your advertisement immediately.

This ebook is not the be all and end all of copywriting. It is enough however, to wet your lips at the exciting income opportunities that effective copywriting can bring.

Testing

Learning to write effecting is a process of trial, error, testing and tracking. Test different headlines. Test different body copy. Test a different price. Test a different list. Test a free premium.

It is suggested to use this material as a reference guide. Study this material. Refer to it often. Write some of the words and phrases on piece of paper and stick them around the house, work area or at least in your computer room. This will help burn the ideas into your being-ness.

You will be surprised at the magic of repeated exposure. The brain only selects information which is of value at a particular time. Repeated exposure to the information will reveal new information with value relevant for that particular time.

Copyright W&S Club (Wealth & Success Club). All rights reserved.

Get Addicted!

Imaging the endless possibilities that will be available to you once you master selling with the printed word. No price is too high if it enables you to live of your dreams. You will then see opportunities almost everywhere continually crossing your path.

The world really is your oyster when you master the art of effective copywriting.

Enjoy...

Copyright W&S Club (Wealth & Success Club). All rights reserved.

Chapter1

The Master Formula

A.I.D.A The Master Formula

The most important aspect of any business is selling the product or service. Without sales, no business can exist for very long.

All sales begin with some form of advertising. To build sales, this advertising must be seen or heard by potential buyers, and cause them to react to the advertising in some way. The credit for the success, the blame for the failure of almost all ads, reverts back to the ad itself.

Generally, the" ad writer" wants the prospect to do one of the following:

- Visit the store to see and judge the product for himself, or immediately write a check and send for the merchandise being advertised

- Phone for an appointment to hear the full sales presentation or write for further information which amounts to the same thing.

The bottom line in any ad is quite simple:

To make the reader buy the product or service! Any ad that causes the reader to only pause in this thinking, to just admire the product, or to simply believe what's written about the product – is **not** doing its job completely.

The "ad writer" must know exactly what he wants his reader to do, and any that does not elicit the desired action is an absolute waste of time and money.

Copyright W&S Club (Wealth & Success Club). All rights reserved.

In order to elicit the desired action from the prospect, all ads are written according to the simple master formula which is called A.I.D.A

- Attract the **attention** your prospect

- **Interest** your prospect in your product

- Cause your prospect to **desire** the product

- Demand **action** from the prospect

Never forget the basic rule of advertising copywriting: if the ad is not read, it won't stimulate any sale; if it is not seen, it cannot be read; and if it does not command or grab the attention of the reader, it will not be seen!

Most successful advertising copywriters knows these fundamentals backwards and forwards

Whether you know them already or you're just now been exposed to them, your knowledge and practice of these fundamentals will determine the extent of your success as an advertising copywriter.

Copyright W&S Club (Wealth & Success Club). All rights reserved.

Chapter2

Classifieds ads

Classified ads are the ads form which all successful businesses are started. These small, relatively inexpensive ads, give the beginner an opportunity to advertise his product or service without losing his shirt if the ad doesn't pull or the people don't break his door down with demands for his product.

Classifieds ads are written according to **all** the advertising rules. What is said in a classified ad is the same that's said in a large, more elaborate type of ad, except in condensed form.

To start learning how to write good classified ads, clip ten classified ads from ten different mail order type publications – ads that you think are pretty good. Paste each of these ads onto a separate sheet of paper.

Analyze each of these ads:

- How has the writer attracted your attention?

- What about the ad keeps you interested?

- Are you stimulated to want to know more about the product being advertised?

- What action must you take?

- Are all of these points covered in the ad?

- How strongly are you "turned on" by each of these ads?

Rate these ads on the scale of one to ten, with ten being the best according to the formula I've given you. Every ad you see from now on, quickly analyze it, and rate it somewhere on your scale. If you will practice this exercise on a regular basis, you will soon be able to quickly recognize the **Power Points** of

Copyright W&S Club (Wealth & Success Club). All rights reserved.

any ad you see, and know within your own mind whether an ad is good, bad or otherwise, and what makes it so.

Practice for an hour each day, writes the ads you've rated 8, 9 and 10 exactly as they've been written. This will give you the **feel** of the fundamentals and style necessary in writing classified ads.

Your next project will be to pick out what you consider to be the **worst** ads you can find in the classifieds sections. Clip these out and paste them onto a sheet of paper so you can work on them.

Read these ads over a couple of some times, and then beside each of them, write a short comment stating why you think it's bad:

- Lost in the crowd, doesn't attract attention?

- Doesn't hold the readers interest?

- Nothing special to make the reader want to own the product?

- No demand for action?

You probably already know what's coming next, and that's right. Break out those pencils, erasers and scratch paper – and start rewriting these ads to include the missing elements.

Each day for the next month, practice writing the ten best ads for an hour, just the way they were originally written. Pick out ten of the worst ads, analyze those ads, and then practice rewriting those until they measure up to doing the job they were intended to do.

Once you're satisfied that the ads you've rewritten are perfect, go back in each ad and cross out the words that can be eliminated without detracting from the ad. Classified ads are almost always **finalized** in the style of a telegram.

Example: I'll arrive at 2 o'clock tomorrow afternoon, the 15th. Meet me at Sardi's. All my love, Jim.

Edited for Sending: Arrive 2pm – 15th – Sardi's. Love, Jim.

Copyright W&S Club (Wealth & Success Club). All rights reserved.

Classified ad: Save on your food bill! Reduced prices on every shelf in the store! Stock up now while suppliers are complete! Come on in today, to Jerry's Family Supermarket!

Edited for Publication: Save on food! Everything bargained priced! Limited suppliers! Hurry! Jerry's markets!

It takes dedicated and regular practice, but you can do it.

Simply recognize and understand the **basic formula** – practice reading and writing the good ones – and rewriting the bad ones to make them better. Practice, and keep at it, over and over, every day – until the formula, the idea, and the feel of this kind of ad writing becomes second nature to you.

Copyright W&S Club (Wealth & Success Club). All rights reserved.

Chapter3

Displayed ads

A display or space ad differs from a classified ad because it has a **headline** and layout and because the style isn't telegraphic. However, the fundamentals of writing the display or space ad are exactly the same as for a classified ad. The basic difference is that you have more room in which to emphasize the master formula.

Most successful copywriters rate the headline and / or the lead sentence of an ad as the **most important** part of the ad, and in reality, you should do the same. After all, when you ad is surrounded by hundreds of other ads, an information or entertainment , what makes you think anyone is going to see your particular ad?

The truth is, they're not going to see your ad unless you can **grab** their attention and entice them to read all of what you have to say. Your headline, or lead sentence when no headline is used, has to make it more difficult for your prospect to ignore or pass over, than to stop and read your ad. If you don't capture the **attention** of your reader with your headline, anything beyond is useless effort and wasted money.

Successful advertising headlines

In classified ad, your first three to five words serve as your headline and are written as promises, either implied or direct.

The former promises to show you how to save money, make money, or attain a desired goal. The latter is a warning against something undesirable.

EXAMPLE OF A PROMISE:

Are You Ready To Become A Millionaire – In Just 18 months?

EXAMPLE OF A WARNING:

Copyright W&S Club (Wealth & Success Club). All rights reserved.

Do You Make These Mistakes in English?

In both of those examples, I've posted a question as a headline. Headlines that ask a question seem to attract the reader's attention almost as surely as a moth is drawn to a flame. Once he's seen the question, he just can't seem to keep himself from reading the rest of the ad to find out the answer. The best headline questions are those that challenge the reader; that involve his self esteem, and do not allow him to dismiss your question with a simple yes or no.

You'll be the envy of your friends is another kind of **reader appeal** to incorporate into your headline whenever appropriate. The appeal has to do with basic psychology: everyone wants to be well thought of, and consequently, will read into the body of your ad to find out how he can gain the respect and accolades his friends.

Wherever and whenever possible, use colloquialisms or words that are not usually found in advertisements. The idea is to shock or shake the reader out of his reverie and cause him to take notice of your ad. Most of the headlines you see day in and day out have certain sameness with just the words rearranged. The reader may see these headlines with his eyes, but his brain fails to focus on any of them because there's nothing different or out of the ordinary to arrest his attention.

EXAMPLE OF QOLLOQUIALISM:

Are You Developing A POT BELLY?

Another attention-grabber kind of headline is the comparative pricegazines, headline: three for only $3, regular $3 each! Still another of the **tried and proven** kind of headlines is the specific question:

Do you suffer from these symptoms?

And of course, if you offer a strong guarantee, you should say so in your headline:

Your Money Refunded, If You Don't Make $100,000 Your First Year.

How To headlines have a very strong basic appeal, but in some instances, they're better used as book titles than advertising headlines.

Copyright W&S Club (Wealth & Success Club). All rights reserved.

Who Else wants in on the finer things – which your product or service presumably offers – is another approach with a very strong appeal. The psychology here is being the need of everyone to belong to a group – complete with a status and prestige motivations.

Whenever, and as often as you can possible work it in. you should use the word **you** in your headline, and throughout the copy. After all, your ad should be directed to **one** person, and the person reading your ad wants to feel that you're talking to him personally, not everyone who lives on his street.

Personalize, and be specific!

You can throw the teachings of your English teachers out of the window, and the rules "third person, singular" or whatever tends to inhabit your writing. Whenever you sit down to write advertising copy intended to pull the orders – sell the product – you should picture yourself in a one – on – one situation and talk to your reader just as if you were sitting across from her at your dinning room table.

Say what you mean, and sell HIM/HER on the product you're offering. Be specific and ask if these are the things that bother her – are these the things she wants – and she's the one you want to buy the product...

The layout you devise for your ad, or the frame you build around it, should also command **attention.**

Either makes it so spectacular that it stands out like lobster at a chili dinner, or so uncommonly simple that it catches the reader's eye because of its very simplicity. It's also important that you don't get cute with a lot of unrelated graphics and artwork. You ad should convey the feeling of excitement and movement, but should not tire the eyes or disrupt the flow of the message you are trying to present.

Any graphics or artwork you use should be relevant to your product, its use and/or the copy you have written about it. Graphics should not be used as artistic touches, or to create an atmosphere. Any illustrations with your ad should complement the selling of your product, and prove or substantiate specific points in your copy.

Once you have your reader's attention, the only way you are going to keep it, is by quickly and emphatically telling him what your product will do for him.

Copyright W&S Club (Wealth & Success Club). All rights reserved.

Your potential buyer doesn't care in the least how long it takes you to produce the product, how lone you have been in business, or how many years you've spend learning your craft. He wants to know specifically how he is going to benefit from the purchase of your product.

Generally, a human wants will fall into one of the following categories:

- Better health

- More comfort

- More money

- More leisure time

- More popularity

- Greater beauty

- Success and/ or security

Even though you have your reader's attention, you must follow through with an enumeration of the benefit you can gain. In essence, you must reiterate the advantages, comfort and happiness she'll enjoy – as you have implied in your headline.

Mentally picture your prospect – determine her wants and emotional needs – put yourself in her shoes, and ask yourself: if I were reading this ad, what are the things that would appeal to me? **Write your copy to appeal to your reader's wants and emotional needs/ ego cravings**

Remember, it's not the "safety features" that have sold cars for the past 50 years – nor has it been the need of transportation – it has been, and almost certainly always will be the advertising writer's recognition of people's **wants and emotional needs/ ego cravings.**

Copyright W&S Club (Wealth & Success Club). All rights reserved.

Visualize your prospect, recognize his wants and satisfy them. Writing good advertising copy is nothing more or less than knowing **who** your buyers are; recognizing what he wants; and then telling him how your product will fulfill each of those wants. Remember this because its one of the **vitally important** keys to writing advertising copy that does the job you intended for it to do.

The **desire** potion of your ad is where you present the facts of your product; create and justify your prospects conviction, and cause him to demand" a piece of the action" for himself.

It's vitally necessary that you present "proven facts" about your product because survey results shows that at least 80% of the people reading your ad – especially those reading it for first time – will tend to question it authenticity.

So, the more fact you can present in the ad, the more credible your offer. As you write this part of your ad, always remember that the more facts about the product you present, the more product you'll sell. People want facts as reasons, and/ or excuses for buying a product – to justify to themselves and others, that they have not been "taken" by a slick copywriter.

It's like a girl who wants to marry the guy her father calls a "no good bum." Her heart – her emotions – tells her eyes, but she needs to nullify the seeds of doubt lingering in her mind – to rationalize her decision to go on with the wedding.

In other words, the **desire** potion of your ad has to build belief and credibility in the mind of your prospect. It has to assure him of his good judgment in the final decision to buy – furnish evidence of the benefits you have promised – and afford him a "safety net" in case anyone should question his decision to buy.

People tend to believe the things that appeal to their individual **desires, fears and other emotions.** Once you have established a belief in this manner, logic and reasoning are used to support it. People believe want they **want** to believe. Your readers **wants** to believe your ad if she has read it through this far – it is up to you to support her initial desire.

Study your product and everything about it – visualize the wants of your prospective buyers – dig up the facts, and you'll almost always find plenty of facts to support the buyer's reasons for buying.

Here is where you use results of tests conducted, growing sales figures to prove increasing popularity, and "user" testimonials or endorsements. It's also

Copyright W&S Club (Wealth & Success Club). All rights reserved.

important that you present these facts – test results, sales view, and not that of the manufacturer.

Before you end this portion of your ad and get into your demand for action, summarize everything you've presented thus so far. Draw a mental picture for your potential buyer. Let him imagine owning the product. Induce him to visualize all of the benefits you have promised. Give him the key to seeing himself richer, enjoying luxury, having time to do whatever he would like to do, and will all of his dreams fulfilled.

This can be handled in one or two sentences, or spelled out in a paragraph or more, but it is the absolute ingredient you must include prior to closing the sale. Study all the sales presentations you have ever heard – look at every winning ad – this is the element included in all of them that actually makes the sales for you. Remember it, use it, and don't try to sell anything without it.

As Victor Schwab puts it so succinctly in his best selling book, How To Write A Good Advertisement:

Every one of the fundamentals in the **master formula** is necessary. Those sitting across from him at your dining people who are '"easy" to sell may perhaps be sold even if some of these factors are left out, but it's wiser to plan your advertisement so that it will have a powerful impact upon those who are "hardest" to sell. For, unlike fact to face selling, we cannot in printed advertising come to a "trail close" in our sales talk – in order to see if those who are easier to sell will welcome the dotted line without further persuasion.

We must assume that we are talking to the hardest ones – and that the more thoroughly our copy sells both the hard and the easy, the better chance we have against the competition for the consumer's dollar – and also the less dependant we will be upon the usual completely ineffective follow through on our advertising effort which later takes place at the sales counter itself.

Ask For Action!

Lots of ads are beautiful, almost perfectly written, and quit convincing – yet they fail to ask for or demand action from the reader. If you want the reader to have your product, then tell her so and demand that she send her money **now.**

Copyright W&S Club (Wealth & Success Club). All rights reserved.

Unless you enjoy entertaining your prospects with your beautiful writing skills, always demand that he/she complete the sales now, by taking action now – by calling a telephone number and ordering, or by writing his check and rushing it to the post office.

Once you have got him on the hook, land him! Don't let him getaway!

Probably, one of the most common and best methods of moving the reader to act now, is written in some form of the following:

- All of these can be your!

- You can start enjoying this new way of life immediately, simply by sending a check for $XXX!

- Don't put it off, then later wish you had gotten in on the ground floor!

- Make out That check now, and "be in on the ground floor!"

- Act now, and as an "early - bird" buyer, you'll include a big bonus package – absolutely free, simply for acting immediately!

- You win all the way! We take all the risk! If you are not satisfied, simply return the product and we will quickly refund your money!

- Do it now! Get that check on its way to us today, and receive the big bonus package!

- After next week, we won't be able to include the bonus as a part of this fantastic deal, so act now!

- The sooner you act, the more you win!

Offering a reward of some kind will almost always stimulate the prospect to take action. However, in mentioning the reward or bonus, be very careful that you don't end up receiving primarily, request for the bonus with mountains with mountains for refunds on the product to follow. The bonus should be only casually if you are asking for product orders; and with lots of fanfare only when you are seeking inquiries.

Copyright W&S Club (Wealth & Success Club). All rights reserved.

Too often the copywriter, in his enthusiasm to pull in a record number of responses, confuses the reader by "forgetting about the product" and devoting his entire space allotted for the "demand for action" to sending for the bonus. Any reward offered should be closely related to the product, and a bonus offered only for immediate action on the part of the potential buyer.

Specify a time limit. Tell your prospect that he must act within a certain time limit or lose out on the bonus, face probably higher prices, or even the withdrawal of your offer. This is always a good hook to get action.

Any kind of guarantee you offer always helps you produce action from the prospect. And the more liberal you can make your guarantee, the more product orders you will receive. Be sure you state the guarantee clearly and simply. Make it so easy to understand that even a child would not misinterpret what you are saying.

The action you want your prospect to take should be easy – clearly stated – and devoid of any complicated procedural steps on her part, or numerous directions for her action to follow.

Picture your prospect, very comfortable in his favorite easy chair, idly flipping through a magazine while "half - watching" TV. He notices your ad, read through it, and he is sold on your product. Now what does he do?

Remember, he's very comfortable – you have **crabbed** his attention, sparked his interest, painted a picture of him enjoying a new kind of satisfaction, and he is ready to buy…

Anything and everything you ask or cause her to do is going to disrupt this aura of comfort and contentment. Whatever she must do had better be simple, quick and easy!

Tell him without any ifs, ands or buts, what to do – fill out the coupon, include your check for the full amount, and send it in to us **today!**

Make it as easy for him as you possible can – simply and direst. And by all means, make sure your address is on the order form he is supposed to complete and mail it to you – your name and address on the order form, as well as just above it. People sometimes fill out the coupon, tear it off, seal it in an envelope and don't know where to send it. The easier you make it for him to respond, the more responses you'll get!

Copyright W&S Club (Wealth & Success Club). All rights reserved.

There you have it, a complete short course on how to write ads that will pull more orders for you – sell of your product for you. It's important to learn **why** ads are written as they are – to understand and use, the **master formula** in you own ad writing endeavors.

By conscientiously studying good advertising copy, and practice in writing ads of your own, now that you have the knowledge and understand what makes advertising copy work, you should be able to quickly develop your copywriting abilities to produce order – pulling ads for your own products.

Even so, and once you do become proficient in writing ads for your own products, you must never stop "noticing" how ads are written, designed and put together by other people. To stop learning would be comparable to shutting off from the rest of the world.

The best ad writers are people in touch with the world in which they live. Every time they see a good ad, they clip it out and save it. Regularly, they pull want makes them good, and why they work.

There's no school in the country that can give you the same kind of education and expertise so necessary in the filed of ad writing.

You must keep yourself up – to – date, aware of, and in - the – know about the other guy – his innovations, style, changes, and the methods he is using to sell his products.

On – the – job training – study and practice – that's what it takes – and if you have got that burning ambition to succeed, you can do it too!

Copyright W&S Club (Wealth & Success Club). All rights reserved.

Chapter4

Power Words

Power Words That Stimulate Emotion and Action

Add sale punch to describe your merchandise or sales offer – use one off the following words.

It may be helpful, used alone, or with other words. They have been selected successful ads for your convenience in preparing copy.

Absolutely ... Anybody ... Announcing ... Amazing ... Approved ... Attractive ... Authentic ...

Bargain ... Beautiful ... Benefit ... Better ... Big ...

Can ... Cash ... Colorful ... Colossal ... Complete ... Confidential ... Crammed...

Delivered ... Desired ... Direct ... Discover ... Discount...

Easily ... Endorsed ... Enormous ... Excellent ... Exciting ... Exclusive ... Expert ...

Famous ... Fascinating ... Fortune ... Free ... Full...

Genuine ... Get ... Gift ... Gigantic ... Greatest ... Guaranteed ...

Helpful ... Highest ... how ... huge ...

Immediately ... Improved ... Informative ... Instructive ... Interesting ... Introducing...

Largest ... Latest ... Lavishly ... Liberal ... Lifetime ... Limited ... Lowest ... Love...

Magic ... Mammoth ... Maximum ... Miracle ...

New ... Noted ... Now...

Copyright W&S Club (Wealth & Success Club). All rights reserved.

Odd ... Opportunity ... Outstanding ...

Personalized ... Popular ... Powerful ... Practical ... Professional ... Profitable ... Profusely ... Proven ...

Quality ... Quickly...

Rare ... Reduced ... Refundable ... Remarkable ... Reliable ... Revealing ... Revolutionary ...

Scare ... Secrets ... security ... Selected ... Sensational ... Simplified ... Sizable... Special... Startling ... Strange ... Strong ... Sturdy ... Successful ... Superior ... Surprise...

Terrific ... Tested ... Today ... Tremendous ...

Unconditional ... Unique ... Unlimited ... Unparalleled ... Unsurpassed ... Unusual ... Useful ...

Valuable ...

Wealth ... Weird ... Win ... Wonderful ...

You ... Your

Copyright W&S Club (Wealth & Success Club). All rights reserved.

Chapter5

Power Phrases

Close your ad with an action – getting phrase. Give the reader something to write or do. Here some suggestions for ways to get action. Study them. They will help you prepare your copy for better results...

- Act Now!
- Send you name...
- All send free to introduce...
- Amazing literature...
- Free...
- Ask for free folder...
- Bargain list send free...
- Be first to qualify...
- Booklet free!
- Catalog included free...
- Complete details free...
- Current list free...
- Dealers write for prices...
- Description send free...
- Details free...
- Everything supplied!
- Exciting details free...
- Folder free!
- For literature, write:
- Free booklet explains...
- Free plans to tell how...
- Free selling kit...
- Free wholesale plan...
- Free with approvals...
- Full particulars free...
- Get facts that help...
- Get started today...
- Get a copy now!
- Get yourself wholesale...

Copyright W&S Club (Wealth & Success Club). All rights reserved.

- Gifts with purchases…
- Illustrated list free…
- Interesting details free…
- Investigate today…
- It's free! Act now!
- Literature free…
- Money making facts free…
- No obligation!
- Write!
- Offer limited!
- Send today…
- Order direct from:
- Order now!
- Particulars free…
- Request free literature…
- Revealing booklet free…
- Sales kit furnished…
- Sample details free…
- Samples send on trials…
- See before you buy…
- Send for free details…
- Send for it today…
- Send no money…
- Send post card today…
- Send today…
- Test lesson free…
- Unique sample offer…
- Valuable details free…
- Write for free booklet free…
- Yours for the asking…
- 32-page catalog free…

Now you have want it takes to master the art of persuasion and communication in the business world, go on make your mark!

Copyright W&S Club (Wealth & Success Club). All rights reserved.

Trainings & Workshops on The Business Art Of Persuasion and Communication:

For Group or One – on – one session on The Business art of persuasion and communication, please contact Us at:
Email: wealthsuccess@zptsotetsi.com

Call Us: +2773 755 1387

Website: http://wealthandsuccess.zptsotetsi.com

   To All Your Success
   W&S Club

Copyright W&S Club (Wealth & Success Club). All rights reserved.

www.ingramcontent.com/pod-product-compliance
Lightning Source LLC
Chambersburg PA
CBHW050944200526
45172CB00020B/1068